THE ALPHA BETA BOOK

Keith U. McCrary

THE ALPHA BETA BOOK

An Introduction to Ancient Greek

by

Keith U. McCrary, BA, MDiv

Waldorf Publications
Research Institute for Waldorf Education

Printed with support from the Waldorf Curriculum Fund

Published by:

Waldorf Publications at the
Research Institute for Waldorf Education
38 Main Street
Chatham, New York 12037

Title: *The Alpha Beta Book:*
An Introduction to Ancient Greek
Author: Keith McCrary
Pictograph illustrations: Keith McCrary
Cover: *A Reading from Homer,* Sir Lawrence Alma-Tadema. Oil on canvas, 1885, 36⅛ × 72¼ inches (91.8 × 183.5 cm), Philadelphia Museum of Art: The George W. Elkins Collection, 1924, permission courtesy of Philadephia Museum of Art
Cover design: Ann Erwin
Copy editor & Layout: Ann Erwin
Proofreader for Ancient Greek: Donald Samson

ISBN # 978-1-936367-41-2
Reprinted 2015

Table of Contents

The Acropolis – Athens, Greece

INTRODUCTION

An Invitation to a Distant Place and Time

Go with me to a distant land, to a land surrounded on three sides by water. Go with me to a distant time, more than two thousand years ago. Go to a time and place where a city was called a πόλις *polis*. One metro*polis* there is named after the Greek goddess of wisdom, Athena. Overlooking Athens is a hill called the Acropolis, where stands the Parthenon, a temple honoring the goddess.

Go with me now down into the city. Wending our way through narrow cobblestone streets, we come to an open market place, called the ἀγορά *agora*. Around the teeming market are public buildings, each with a large covered porch called a στόα *stoa*. There you will find many citizens gathered, seriously discussing philosophy. In fact, one group of philosophers is called *Stoics* after the *stoa* where they met and developed their philosophy.

Some here are quoting Socrates, saying, Γνῶθι Σαυτόν *Gnōthi Sauton*, which in English means "Know Thyself," a profound and challenging bit of wisdom. Say it after me: [Gnōthee Sowtŏn]. Know thyself. You might also hear: Μηδὲν Ἄγαν *Mēden Agan*, which means "Nothing in Excess." This expresses the philosopher Aristotle's view on the importance of balance in life. Pronounce it [Māden Agän]. Nothing in excess.

You might ask: What is philosophy? Simply put, it means the "love of wisdom." It comes from two Greek words: *philia* meaning "love" and *sophia* meaning "wisdom." It is wise not to do anything excessively, and it is wise to know who you are.

In the agora school children gather around a pedagogue (a tutor, literally "a leader of children"). With him they will learn much, including their letters. Let's listen in. Say it with them as best you can. It's easy: *alpha, beta, gamma, delta, epsilon, zeta, eta, theta, iota, kappa, lambda, mu, nu, xi, omicron, pi, rho, sigma, tau, upsilon, phi, chi, psi, omega.*

Reconstruction: Nashville, TN

The Parthenon

Rendering by Gorham P. Stevens, 1938

1.
WHY STUDY ANCIENT GREEK?

Here is an attempt to put a beginning knowledge of Ancient Greek in the hands of anyone interested. Why bother? What is the value of studying Ancient Greek? There are many good answers. Here are several.

1. Ancient Greek is one of the great formative languages of the world. Greek came from the same root source from which Latin emerged: Indo-European. Thus they share many of the same words. Ancient Greek's presence is in German, in the Scandinavian languages, the Romance languages and, of course, in English. Ancient Greek also influenced the written form of a number of languages. For example, you can see some of the same letters in the Russian alphabet.

Over seventy percent of the English language is derived from Ancient Greek and Latin! Thus, to have a deeper understanding of our language, Ancient Greek is extremely helpful. A lot of our large words (polysyllabic ones) come from Ancient Greek. Almost all of our medical and legal words come from Latin or Greek or both.

2. Knowing some Ancient Greek can aid in spelling correctly. For example, "pneumonia" is a common spelling bee challenge. Originally in Greek the *p* was pronounced, but for us now, it is silent. We have to learn it as a "sight word" in addition to its phonetic clues. It helps to know that "breath" in Ancient Greek is *pneuma*. Unfortunately, the disease <u>pneum</u>onia affects the breath in a negative way. Fortunately *pneuma* shows up in other words. <u>Pneuma</u>tic tires contain air. Pneumatic pumps and drills use compressed air (breath) in their machines.

In Greek mythology Mnemosyne was not only the mother of the Muses, but she was also the goddess of memory. Thus a <u>mnemo</u>nic device is a way of remembering something. Like the silent *p* in "pneumonia," the *m* is silent and so the word begins with the sound of the letter *n*. This should be helpful for remembering how to spell the word correctly. "Amnesia" is, of course, a related word meaning "no memory." I hope you will remember this.

3. Much like the study of one's own family history, when learning Ancient Greek we gain an appreciation of our language's roots and the cultural heritage interwoven with them. It is "a getting in touch with" one's ancestors, our great grandmothers and great grandfathers, our distant relatives—linguistically speaking.

4. The study of Ancient Greek can aid in appreciating the mystery of language itself. How it is translated, transliterated, and transformed into other languages can be revealing. A transliteration is writing out in the letters of one alphabet into the letters of another alphabet, as we do when we change Ancient Greek into English, for example βῆτα transliterates into *beta.*

When we say: "It's lost in the translation," that is only partly true. Something can be gained when the human imagination is at work changing words into different expressions, including transliterations. New insights can unfold; richer, fuller meanings can emerge.

5. For some people, a minor, yet good, reason to have at least a familiarity with the Greek alphabet is that it can come in handy in playing Scrabble. Especially if you get the *x*, the Greek letter *xi* can be spelled out and can even score well if placed in the right spot. All of the other Greek letters are allowed as well, according to *The Official Scrabble Players Dictionary*. Similarly, crossword puzzles occasionally ask for Greek letters spelled out in English.

6. The most obvious and indeed the most significant value for absorbing something of this ancient language is the expansion of one's vocabulary. It has been clearly documented that those students having a knowledge of Ancient Greek score higher on SAT exams and the like. They simply have a larger vocabulary or can figure out the meaning of words they don't know from knowing the Greek origins. (This little book might help a student preparing for such a standardized test.)

7. Along with expanding one's vocabulary, this endeavor also can enrich one's involvement with the English language. For over thirty years I have introduced fifth grade students in various Waldorf schools to Ancient Greek. On the first day of class, after reciting the Greek alphabet a few times, I ask the question: "What is one word you know that comes from Ancient Greek?" Someone always answers "alphabet" because it comes from the first two letters of the Greek alphabet: *alpha beta*. Then there is an immediate "aha" from the whole class. Wonder comes alive, and the students are curious to learn more.

In what follows I hope to lead you into this experience often. It is my sincere hope that this work will soon enable you to decipher words you might not have known before. I hope you will come to enjoy the English language more by learning about the origins of words you already know.

For the teacher and for the parent teaching his or her child, this book can be a manual. It can help you expand the vocabularies of those you teach. For the adventurous, motivated student, it can be a self-help book. The accompanying CD can be a fun and invaluable aid as well.

We use the famous phrase "It's Greek to me" to refer to something one does not understand. Perhaps this offering will modify that statement for you. With a basic grasp of this seminal language, many things will become understandable because it *IS* Greek to you.

2.
THE FUN OF LEARNING TO SAY THE GREEK ALPHABET

A natural beginning point for introducing Ancient Greek is the alphabet. Moreover, most every student I have taught has enjoyed the process of memorizing the Greek alphabet. This has been true largely because of the way we do it. I have included here some of those methods used successfully over the years with my students.

Here is the alphabet transliterated into English, with pronunciation clues in brackets. I will expand on this as we go along, but let's have some fun getting started. Read the pairs across from left to right.

ALPHA [älfä]	>	BETA [bātä]
GAMMA [gämmä]	>	DELTA [dĕltä]
EPSILON [ĕpsilŏn]	>	ZETA [dzātä]
ETA [ātä]	>	THETA [thātä]
IOTA [eeōtä]	>	KAPPA [käppä]
LAMBDA [lämdä]	>	MU [moo]
NU [noo]	>	XI [ksee]
OMICRON [ŏmikrŏn]	>	PI [pea]
RHO [hrō]	>	SIGMA [sigmä]
TAU [täō]	>	UPSILON [oopsilŏn]
PHI [fee]	>	CHI [khee]
PSI [psee]	>	OMEGA [ōmĕgä]

You can memorize this alphabet in a short time. Just follow these suggestions. First, simply read through the twenty-four letters three times just to get your tongue around the sounds.

Now, read them rhythmically. One of the best ways to memorize the Greek alphabet (and many other things) is by using different speech rhythms—and then moving to the sounds while speaking them. For example, the list of Greek letters written above has been purposely placed in pairs. This will make it easy to say the letters with a two-beat rhythm. Try saying it that way: *alpha beta / gamma delta / epsilon zeta / eta theta / iota kappa / lambda mu / nu xi / omicron pi / rho sigma / tau upsilon / phi chi / psi omega.*

Next, step to that rhythm and say the alphabet at the same time. If you are unable to step for some reason, clapping or tapping is fine.

After that has been practiced three or four times, try a three-beat rhythm: *alpha beta gamma / delta epsilon zeta / eta theta iota / kappa lambda mu / nu xi omicron / pi rho sigma / tau upsilon phi / chi psi omega.* Then do it again, moving to that rhythm and saying the alphabet at the same time.

Because the Greek alphabet has twenty-four letters, rhythms of four, six, eight, and even twelve can be used. You may want to count on your fingers to keep track with four or more beats. Continue to move to the rhythms whenever possible.

Now that you have begun to get the hang of rhythmic moving and speaking, I recommend beginning the process over again with the following sequence:

1. Read the alphabet again, straightforwardly.

2. Now put your thumbs in your belt, waist, or pockets, and then bow your legs a bit like a cowboy or cowgirl. Move up and down in place like you are riding a horse as you say the alphabet with a two-beat rhythm and the best Texas accent you can muster. You don't have to keep a straight face—unless you are from Texas.

3. This can be varied with any of the following accents: Mexican, aristocratic English, French, and Italian (with lively hand gestures). The three-beat rhythm seems to work well with the foreign accents.

Notice how one's posture shifts with different accents. A person usually stands or sits up straighter when using a British accent.

Be creative. Use any other accents or voices you might have at your command.

4. You can also impersonate famous characters or actors saying the alphabet, if you have such in your repertoire. Many of my students have had fun trying to say the alphabet with a voice similar to an animated cartoon character named Droopy.

5. Another fun variation can be used when you have complete command in reciting the alphabet: See how fast you can say it. Use a stopwatch to time yourself. Anything under ten seconds is commendable. The record to date, in my experience, is six seconds. Group efforts have accomplished it in as few as seven seconds.

6. Finally, try singing the Greek alphabet to the tune of "Twinkle, Twinkle Little Star," the traditional alphabet song. It does work. The alphabet is even easier to learn if you say/sing it with another person—or more.

I have used these methods effectively in classes for many years. Students have come up to me years later to tell me that they still recall the alphabet—and then they go on to prove it in the seconds that follow.

The Alpha Beta Song*

*to the tune of "Twinkle, Twinkle Little Star"

Pronunciation Guide

Letter in transliteration	Sound	Pronunciation	As in
a	broad	[ä]	father
e	short	[ĕ]	enter
ē	long	[ā]	they
i	short	[ĭ]	it
	long	[ee]	fee
o	short	[ŏ]	moss
ō	long	[ō]	most
u, y		[oo]	oops!
th		[th]	theta
rh		[hr]	rhythm
ph		[f]	phone
ch		[kh]	loch
ps		[ps]	apse
z		[dz]	adze
x		[ks]	axiom
gg		[ng]	song
ai		[ī]	aisle
au		[ow]	cow
ei		[ā]	weigh
eu		[ĕū]	feud
oi		[oy]	oil, boy
ou		[oo]	moo

Some pronunciation tips

In going through the alphabet, you may have already noticed the pronouncing of certain Greek letters is different from what you might have heard before. This is due, in part, to scholars and fraternity/ sorority organizations who use alternative or modernized pronunciations. However, since we want to get it right, here are some pointers:

The ending *a* in *alpha, beta, gamma, delta*, and so on, requires a broad or open *a* sound, as in "father," indicated with [ä].

Epsilon's *e* is short [ĕ], as in "enter."

The *e* in *eta* is pronounced as a long *a* [ā]. The same is true for *beta, zeta* and *theta*.

Mathematicians have long used the Greek letter *pi* to represent the number 3.14 (approximately), which has to do with figuring the distance around a circle ($C = \pi d$) and the area of a circle ($A = \pi r^2$). In math classes the letter is usually pronounced "pie." However, in Greek (ancient and modern), it is pronounced "pea," as in the little green vegetable.

The letter *phi* should also be pronounced with the same long *e* sound: [ee]. The founders of Phi Beta Kappa, the honorary academic fraternity/sorority, should have known better than to pronounce it "fie." Fie on them! Just kidding. Similarly, *iota* = [eeōtä], *xi* = [ksee], *chi* = [khee], and *psi* = [psee] use a long *e* sound.

Both letters *o* in *omicron* are short [ŏ], as in "moss." The long *o* sound comes with the *omega*.

The *u* in *upsilon, mu* and *nu* is pronounced [oo] as in "oops." Oops, I hope this part isn't too complicated or tiresome.

The *g* sound in *gamma* is the hard *g* as in "great." The single *g* is always hard. When two gammas are together, you get a "ng" sound as in "song."

Two extra vowels

The vowels in Ancient Greek are essentially parallel to those in English: A E I O U equals *alpha, epsilon, iota, omicron*, and *upsilon*. The Greek alphabet, however, has two more: *eta* and *omega*.

Eta is pronounced with a long *a* [ātä], as we have already noted. The combination *ei* also makes the long *a* sound, as in the Greek word for the number "one": εἷς *heis*, which is pronounced [hās or hāce], to which our word "ace" is related.

As already noted, the *omega* in Greek makes a long *o* sound, as in a word like "most." For pronouncing the long *o*, we will use [ō].

Note: *Eta* is transliterated as ē (pronounced ā), to differentiate it from *epsilon (e)*, and *omega* is transliterated as ō, to differentiate it from *omicron (o)*.

Squiggles: breathing marks and accents

When a Greek word begins with a vowel, there is an apostrophe over the vowel to indicate pronunciation. If the apostrophe is pointing to the left ('), the vowel is pronounced on its own normally. This is called a "smooth breathing." If the apostrophe is facing the opposite way (ʽ), one must add an *h* sound [h] before the vowel. This is called a "rough breathing."

The Greeks did not have an *h* in their alphabet, so they used this rough breathing symbol of the backward apostrophe to indicate that sound. (Do not be confused when you see the capital letter *eta*: It looks just like a capital *H* but it is still pronounced as a long *a* [ā], as in "bay.")

Ancient Greek also uses accent marks. They included them in the normal presentation of their words, not just in parentheses in the dictionary as is done in English. They are used to indicate which syllable to stress. The accent is always over the vowel in the stressed syllable. When the vowel is short, it is marked with an acute (´); when the vowel is long, it is marked with a circumflex (῀). When the last syllable in a word is stressed and followed by another word, it is marked with a grave (`).

This may seem like a lot to keep track of, but you will find that once you get going with actual words and phrases, it will all become easier. In the next part of this book, we will continue to work with the letters, but with an emphasis on expanding one's vocabulary. As you will see, many of the words we already know in the English language are derived from Ancient Greek.

Aspirations and double-letter sounds

There are seven letters in Ancient Greek that deserve special attention because all seven require two letters in English to represent them. Four of these letters are what we call aspirated letters, which means we add a [h] sound to the letter. *Theta* θ is pronounced [th]. *Phi* φ is pronounced [f], and *rho* ρ is pronounced [hr]. *Chi* χ is pronounced with a sound we don't use in English; it is like the *ch* in the Scottish word "loch" and is represented in this book with [kh].

The three other letters are double-letter sounds: *Zeta* ζ begins with a [d] sound preceding the *z*, pronounced as in "adze," the wood-carving tool. *Xi* ξ always makes the sound of [ks], and *psi* ψ makes a [ps] sound.

Diphthongs

We call the sound formed by the combination of two vowels a diphthong. Pronunciation guides are given for these combinations in the chart on page 16.

The Greek Alphabet

Α Β Γ Δ Ε Ζ Η Θ Ι Κ Λ Μ Ν Ξ Ο Π Ρ Σ Τ Υ Φ Χ Ψ Ω

α β γ δ ε ζ η θ ι κ λ μ ν ξ ο π ρ σ τ υ φ χ ψ ω

				Transliteration			
Α	α	ΑΛΦΑ	ἄλφα	*alpha*	A	a	drama
Β	β	ΒΗΤΑ	βῆτα	*bēta*	B	b	bible
Γ	γ	ΓΑΜΜΑ	γάμμα	*gamma*	G	g, ng	going
Δ	δ	ΔΕΛΤΑ	δέλτα	*delta*	D	d	decalog
Ε	ε	ΕΨΙΛΟΝ	ἔψιλον	*epsilon*	E	e	epic
Ζ	ζ	ΖΗΤΑ	ζῆτα	*zēta*	Z	z	adze
Η	η	ΗΤΑ	ἦτα	*ēta*	E	ē	they
Θ	θ	ΘΗΤΑ	θῆτα	*thēta*	Th	th	atheist
Ι	ι	ΙΩΤΑ	ἰῶτα	*iōta*	I	i	intrigue
Κ	κ	ΚΑΠΠΑ	κάππα	*kappa*	K	k	crisis
Λ	λ	ΛΑΜΒΔΑ	λάμβδα	*lambda*	L	l	logic
Μ	μ	ΜΥ	μῦ	*mu*	M	m	meter
Ν	ν	ΝΥ	νῦ	*nu*	N	n	anti
Ξ	ξ	ΞΙ	ξῖ	*xi*	X	x	axiom
Ο	ο	ΟΜΙΚΡΟΝ	ὄμικρον	*omicron*	O	o	moss
Π	π	ΠΙ	πῖ	*pi*	P	p	poet
Ρ	ρ	ΡΩ	ῥῶ	*rhō*	Rh, rh, r		rhythm
Σ	σ, ς	ΣΙΓΜΑ	σίγμα	*sigma*	S	s	spore
Τ	τ	ΤΑΥ	ταῦ	*tau*	T	t	tone
Υ	υ	ΥΨΙΛΟΝ	ὑψιλόν	*upsilon*	Y	y, u	hoops
Φ	φ	ΦΙ	φῖ	*phi*	Ph	ph	Philip
Χ	χ	ΧΙ	χῖ	*chi*	Ch	ch	loch
Ψ	ψ	ΨΙ	ψῖ	*psi*	Ps	ps	maps
Ω	ω	ΩΜΕΓΑ	ὠμέγα	*ōmega*	O	ō	ocean

3.
Increasing Your Vocabulary with Greek Letters and Words

In many Greek words the relationship to English words is obvious, as in "alphabet." Others are not so apparent. For example, *hippos* means "horse"; *potamos* means "river." Together they make *hippopotamus,* a "river horse."

By using artwork in the process of learning the letters, the feeling life of the students becomes engaged along with the intellect and can make a significant difference in remembering what is presented. The emotional aspect can also serve as a bridge between the intellect and the will, thus involving the whole person. Making drawings and/or doing writing has a deepening effect upon the student trying to learn the alphabet. When this takes place, remembering the content is much more likely to be successful.

On the following pages the Greek letters are hidden in a series of drawings called pictographs. Your job is to find them. Even better—make your own little Greek book. Feel free to copy the illustrations presented in this book. This is what my students have done. Then if you like, you may circle or outline your discoveries with a highlighter or colored pencil to indicate the location of each Greek letter. This can help in recognizing and recalling the forms of the letters.

Besides the Ancient Greek words introduced, their meanings have been included along with one or more derivatives.

To get you started on your search for the hidden Greek letters, here are two clues. In the *alpha* illustration, look for the letter form in the head of the angel. In the *beta* illustration find the *beta* on the right side of the four-leaf clover. Use your imagination as you look for the other twenty-two.

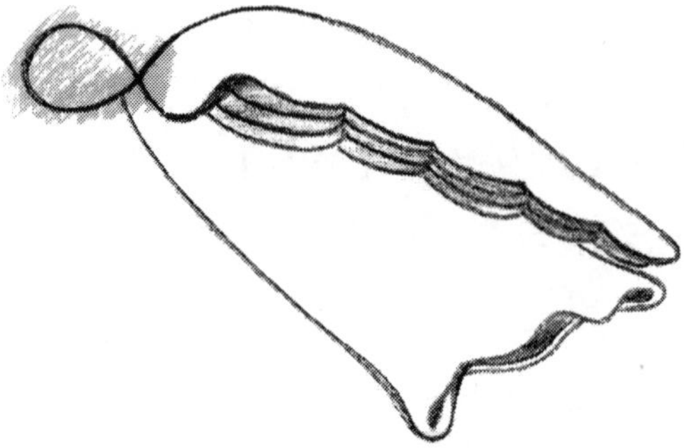

ΑΛΦΑ ἄλφα
ALPHA Α α

Alpha is for *angelos* [ängelŏs], as in angel. It also appears in Los Angeles, "The City of Angels." The Greek word means "messenger," so it shows up in our word evangelist, a person who is said to bring a good message or good news.

In Ancient Greek *akros* [äkrŏs] means "summit, top" or "heights." Overlooking the capital of Greece, the city of Athens, is a famous site called the Acropolis, where a great temple was built to honor the goddess Athena. The Greek word for city is πόλις *polis* [pŏlis], as in our word metropolis. So Acropolis means, literally, "above the city." Where else does *akros* show up in English? Imagine a tight rope walker or a trapeze artist doing tricks high above a circus crowd. He or she is called an _____. That's right: an acrobat, originally someone who performed from a place high overhead. You wouldn't want to be an acrobat if you have acrophobia, a fear of heights.

ἄκρος *akros* [äkrŏs] = summit, top ~ acrobat
Ἀκρόπολις *Akropolis* [äkrŏpŏlis] ~ Acropolis
ἄγγελος *angelos* [ängelŏs] = messenger ~ angel, evangelism
ἀντί *anti* [äntee] = opposite, in place of ~ antibiotic
ἀστήρ *astēr* [ästār] = star ~ astronomy
αὐτός *autos* [owtŏs] = self ~ automatic, automobile

BHTA βῆτα
BETA B β

The Greek word for "life" is *bios* [beeŏs]. Biology is the study of life. One major branch of biology is botany, the study of plants. As clover is a form of plant life, I have used it to introduce the letter *beta*.

What do we call the written story of a person's life? You are right if you said: "biography." Other words related to *bios* include bionic, biosphere, and biodegradable and biofeedback.

To the Ancient Greeks, the language of foreigners sounded like "bar-bar-bar," and so they became known as *barbaros* [bärbärŏs], which meant someone who didn't speak Greek, thus a foreigner. From this we get the words barbarian and barbarous, meaning primitive in culture and customs.

Biblion [bibliŏn], meaning "book," appears in English in the word Bible and in the Spanish and German words for "library": *biblioteca* and *bibliothek*, respectively. A bibliography is a list of reference books often found at the end of a scholarly paper or book.

The word for "cow" in Ancient Greek is *bous* [boos], from which we get the word "bovine," having to do with cows, oxen, and so forth. This word appears in a short, humerous poem, "The Cow" by Ogden Nash. Poetry that depicts country life, where a herdsman of cows lives and works, is called bucolic poetry.

βάρβαρος *barbaros* [bärbärŏs] = foreign ~ barbarian, barbaric
βίβλιον *biblion* [bibliŏn] = book ~ bibliography, Bible
βίος *bios* [beeŏs] = life ~ biology, biography
βοῦς *bous* [boos] = cow ~ bovine
βουκόλος *boukolos* [bookŏlŏs] = cowherd ~ bucolic

ΓΑΜΜΑ γάμμα
GAMMA Γ γ

Note the old-fashioned quill pen. Can you see the shape of the lower case *gamma* in it as well as what the quill has written? The Greek word for "writing" is *gramma* [grämä]. Besides being related to grammar, it is connected to grammarian, telegram, gramophone, anagram, and diagram.

In our time when people are living longer than they used to, doctors and nurses have begun to study the aging process. To describe the medical practice of treating the elderly, they borrowed from the Greek word for "old age," *gēras* [gāräs] and coined the word geriatrics.

Another word beginning with *gamma* which certainly deserves noting is the goddess *Gaia* [Gīä]. She is commonly called Mother Earth. From *Gaia* we get geology, geography, geode, and the names Georgia and George.

Γαῖα *Gaia* [Gīä] = Gaia, mother of the Titans
γῆ *gē* [gā] = earth ~ geology
γένος *genos* [genŏs] = birth ~ genes, Genesis
γῆρας *gēras* [gāräs] = old age ~ geriatrics
γράμμα *gramma* [grämä] = writing ~ grammar, telegram
γράφω *grapho* [gräfō] = to draw, write ~ graphics, graphite, geography

ΔΕΛΤΑ δέλτα
DELTA Δ δ

When it came to describing the silty deposit at the mouth of a river, someone noticed that the flow of water creates a triangular-shaped landform—like the shape of the Greek capital letter *delta*. Two of the most famous deltas are the Nile Delta in Egypt and the Mississippi Delta in Louisiana. It was in that state that Delta Airlines had its beginnings. The airline still uses a stylized shape of this Greek letter as its logo.

In the human body there is a shoulder muscle that has this same form. It is called the deltoid muscle. Look in a mirror at your bare shoulder, and you can see it. The tip of the triangular form is pointing downward between the biceps and triceps.

δεσπότης *despotēs* [despŏtās] = dictator ~ despot
δῆμος *dēmos* [dāmŏs] = the people ~ democracy
δύναμις *dynamis* [doonämis] = power ~ dynamic, dynamite

ΕΨΙΛΟΝ ἔψιλον
EPSILON Ε ε

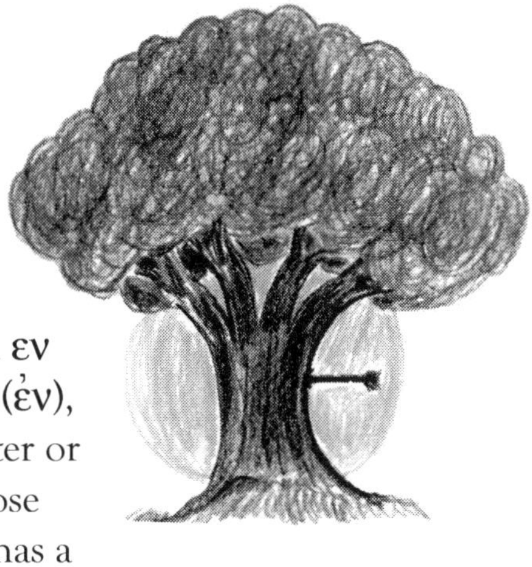

Look for the lower case *epsilon* in the lower part of the tree—with the arrow in it.

There are two Greek words spelled εν *en*. One has a smooth breathing mark (ἐν), is pronounced with a short *e*, as in enter or entrance, and means "in, on." Yes, those are also derivatives. The second form has a rough breathing mark (ἕν). This calls for an *h* sound before the vowel and is pronounced [hĕn]. It is a Greek word for the number "one."

In the section on the numerals you will find that the number eleven is a combination of *hen* and δέκα *deka* (ten): ἕνδεκα *hendeka*. The rim of the Susan B. Anthony dollar coin is a hendecagon, an eleven-sided figure, used here to commemorate the flight of Apollo 11 pictured on the back. There is even a hendecasyllabic meter in poetry that has eleven syllables per line. The Greeks of old and the Romans, especially Catullus, used this form, as did some modern poets, including Alfred Lord Tennyson and Robert Frost.

Our word "ego" comes directly from the Greek word *egō* [ĕgō] for "I" or "one's self." If a person has a big ego, we call that person an egotist or describe him or her as egotistical. Egotism can be one of the bigger problems in human relations—when people think too highly of themselves and their opinions.

The little Greek word *eu* [ĕū] meaning "good," often appears as a prefix in English, as in eulogy, good words spoken or written in tribute to someone, commonly at a funeral or memorial service. *Eu* is also in the word euphemism, an inoffensive term substituted for one considered blunt or offensive. Eugene and Eugenia mean "well born." (See *genos* above, having to do with "birth" and "beginnings.") "Good rhythm" is implied in the word eurythmy. Euphony is sound that is agreeable, and euphoria is a sense of great well-being.

Epi [ĕpee], meaning "upon" or "around," is another word that usually appears as a prefix. *Derma* δέρμα means "skin." Your epidermis is your outer skin on top of the layer of skin that is "inside or within," which is called the endodermis. *Dēmos* δῆμος means "community, people." An epidemic is an infectious disease that has an effect upon a whole community.

ἐγώ *egō* [ĕgō] = I, self ~ ego, egotism
ἔθος *ethos* [ĕthŏs] = custom, habit ~ ethics
ἐπί *epi* [ĕpee] = upon, around ~ epidermis, EpiPen®, epiphany
εὖ *eu* [ĕū] = good ~ eulogy, euphoria, eurythmy

ZHTA ζῆτα
ZETA Z ζ

The capital Greek letter *zeta* is just like our capital Z. You'll find its form in the pictograph of lightning, which refers to Zeus in Greek mythology, the king of the Greek gods and thrower of lightning bolts. Of course, his name begins with *zeta*. Remember to add a *d* sound when using his name while speaking Greek: Ζεύς [dzĕūs]. If the *z* were removed, we have the word *deus*, the Latin word for "a god, a deity." In Spanish it is *Dios*. In French, *Dieux*. These last two words also appear in their expressions for goodbye: *adios* and *adieu*, "go with God."

Zoon [dzŏ'ŏn], the Greek word for "animal," shows up in our words "zoo," where a zoologist could study animals (zoology). In the sky we have a circle of constellations, many of which have animal forms. We call it the zodiac.

Zephyros [dzefoorŏs] was the god of the west wind, characterized as a gentle breeze (in contrast to Boreas, the god of the north wind, who could be cold and violent). The word "zephyr" has been borrowed since ancient times by musicians, authors, car and motorcycle manufacturers (Ford and Kawasaki), as well as by aviation, naval, and train companies. Why do you suppose they use this word?

Zōnē [dzōnā], Greek for "girdle" or "belt," is obviously related to our word zone.

ζῆλος *zēlos* [dzālŏs] = zeal for ~ zealous, jealous
Ζέφυρος *Zephyros* [dzefoorŏs] = Zephyr, god of the west wind
ζώνη *zōnē* [dzōnā] = girdle, belt ~ zone
ζῷον *zoon* [dzŏ'ŏn] = animal ~ zoo, zoology, zodiac

HTA ἦτα
ETA H η

The pictograph is one of the infant Heracles, whose name means "the glory of Hera," wife of Zeus and queen of the Greek gods. Even as a baby, his strength was extraordinary: When a jealous Hera sent two snakes into his crib to kill him, he simply squeezed them to death. Look for the lower case *eta* in the snakes and in Heracles's strong shoulder and bicep. The Greek word *hērōs* [hārōs] means "demi-god" and Heracles, the son of Zeus and a mortal, was one, for sure. He was notable for feats of strength and courage. From *hērōs* we get hero and heroine.

Another god in Greek mythology, *Hēlios* [Hāleeŏs], the sun god, is often pictured as driving a four-horse chariot pulling the sun across the sky. From his name comes helium, a gas that makes up about one-third of the sun. When astronomers describe our solar system with all the planets orbiting the sun in the center, they call it heliocentric—in contrast to the geocentric theory, that the sun and planets circle the earth.

The Greek word for "pleasure" is ἡδονή *hēdonē* [hādŏnā]. Although the Greeks used the *eta* for the long *a*, when it morphs into English, it often becomes a long *e* as in hedonist, a person who overindulges in pleasure.

Hēmisus [hāmisoos], meaning "half," shows up in our word hemisphere, as in the Northern Hemisphere, the half of the earth above the Equator. A hemitone is an alternative musical term for a half-tone, a pitch interval halfway between two whole tones.

ἦθος *ēthos* [āthŏs] = custom ~ ethics, ethos
ἥλιος *hēlios* [hāleeŏs] = sun ~ helium
ἥμισυς *hēmisus* [hāmisoos] = half ~ hemisphere
ἥρως *hērōs* [hārōs] = hero, demigod ~ hero, heroine, heroic

ΘΗΤΑ θῆτα
THETA Θ θ

The capital letter *theta* is represented as the shield of the Greek soldier in the pictograph, protecting his chest. The word for that part of the human body in Ancient Greek is *thōrax*, and has come directly into English to mean that part of the human anatomy. As an adjective one can speak of the thoracic cavity, within which reside the lungs and heart.

Theos [thĕŏs] is the word for "god" in Ancient Greek. In modern English theology is the study of God, the Bible, other Holy Scriptures, and related topics. When combined with the Greek word for "gift," δώρον *dōron* [dōrŏn], the names Theodore, Theodora, and Dorothy mean "gift of God." *Theos* also appears in a subtle yet profound way in the word "enthusiasm." It is there in the "thus" part of the word, suggesting that when you are enthusiastic about something, you have God or Spirit within you.

Thermos [thermŏs], meaning "hot," has also come directly into our language to refer to a container that can keep its contents hot or warm. What word do we use to measure one's body temperature? Yes, it's a thermometer. Here are some other ways this Greek relative shows up in English: thermostat, thermal underwear (to keep the body warm), and rising warm air in the atmosphere is called a thermal. Thermodynamics is the study of heat in relation to other forms of energy.

θεός *theos* [thĕŏs] = god ~ theology, enthusiasm, atheist
θεραπεύω *therapeuo* [therăpĕūō] = to care for ~ therapy
θερμός *thermos* [thermŏs] = hot ~ thermometer, thermal
θώραξ *thōrax* [thōrăks] = *chest* ~ thoracic

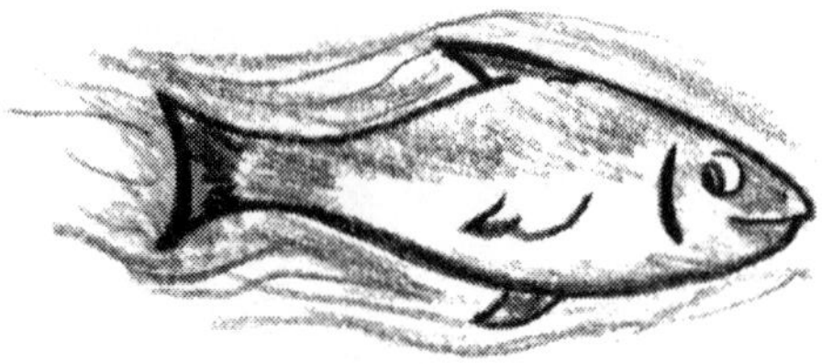

ΙΩΤΑ ἰῶτα
IOTA Ι ι

The word *ichthus* [ikhthoos] in Greek means "fish." The study of fish is called ichthyology. The lower case *iōta* is much like the shape of the gill on the fish.

The Greek word *idea* means "form" or "pattern, and it has come directly into English as idea. Closely related, the Greek verb "to see" is *idein*, from which we derive ideal and idealism.

In Ancient Greek the word for "layman" or "person lacking in skill or expertise" was ἰδιώτης *idiōtes* [ideeōtās], from which we get idiot. Interestingly, *idiōtes* derived from a similar yet distinct Greek word, *idios,* which means "peculiar" or "private." A peculiar habit can be called an idiosyncrasy, and an unusual pattern of behavior can be described as idiosyncratic.

As indicated earlier, one of the most interesting combinations of Greek words is "horse": *hippos* [hippŏs] and "river": ποταμός *potamos* [pŏtămŏs]. From them we get hippopotamus, a river horse.

A narrow strip of land is called an *isthmos* [isthmŏs]. From it we get the word isthmus as in the Isthmus of Panama and the Isthmus of Corinth.

ἰδέα *idea* [ideā] = form, pattern ~ idea
ἰδεῖν *idein* [idān] = to see ~ idea, ideal
ἴδιος *idios* [ideeŏs] = one's own, private ~ idiosyncracy, idiom
ἵππος *hippos* [hippŏs] = horse ~ hippodrome
ἰσθμός *isthmos* [isthmŏs] = narrow strip of land
ἰχθύς *ichthus* [ikhthoos] = fish ~ ichthyology

ΚΑΠΠΑ κάππα
KAPPA Κ κ

Kardia [kardeeä] is the Ancient Greek word for "heart." A heart attack can be called a cardiac arrest. A cardiologist is a doctor who specializes in the care of the heart. An electrocardiograph (EKG) measures the electrical activity in the heart.

The word for "head" in Greek is *kephalē* [kĕfälā]. Encephalitis is an inflammation of the brain. A hydrocephalic is a person with an excess of water on the brain. An octopus with its large head and eight legs belongs to the family of sea creatures called cephalopods.

Kleptēs [kleptās] is Ancient Greek for "thief." A person who steals compulsively is called a kleptomaniac.

The word for "universe" in Ancient Greek is *kosmos* [kŏsmŏs]. From it we get such words as cosmic, cosmology, cosmopolitan," and cosmos itself.

Kryptō [krooptō] involves "hiding" something. A crypt is a tomb that is commonly put in the underground or basement level of a church. In making a cryptic remark, a person is hiding the meaning from some people. Cryptography has to do with making or breaking codes, hidden messages.

καρδια *kardia* [kardeeä] = heart ~ cardiac
κεφαλή *kephalē* [kĕfälā] = head ~ encephalitis
κλέπτης *kleptēs* [kleptās] = thief ~ kleptomaniac
κοσμέω *kosmeō* [kŏsmĕō] = to arrange, adorn ~ cosmetics
κόσμος *kosmos* [kŏsmŏs] = universe ~ cosmos
κρύπτω *kryptō* [krooptō] = hiding ~ crypt, cryptography

ΛΑΜΒΔΑ λάμβδα
LAMBDA Λ λ

Look for the lower case *lambda* in the mouth of the lion, or in Greek: *leōn* [lĕōn].

The word for "stone" in Ancient Greek is *lithos* [lithŏs]. It comes into English in the word lithography, a printing process in which an image was originally rendered on a smooth stone. The Paleolithic Age points to the "old" Stone Age when humans used rough or chipped stone tools. The Neolithic Age refers to a "new" Stone Age time when polished stone tools were used.

Many English words end in "-logy." They are all related to the Greek word *logos* [lŏgŏs, though it is often pronounced lōgōs]. It can be translated as "word" or "reason" or "meaning." So biology literally means the words about life. The words about the earth can be found in the study of geology. Logic is another derivative. *The Gospel of St. John* opens with the following sentence: "In the beginning was the Word." The word for "Word" in the Greek passage is *Logos.*

Lyra [loorä] is the Greek word for "harp" and is also the name of a starry constellation that looks a bit like one. Our words lyre, lyrics, lyricist, and lyrical are all related to it.

λαμπάς *lampas* [lämpäs] = torch ~ lamp
λέων *leōn* [lĕōn] = lion ~ Leo, leonine
λίθος *lithos* [lithŏs] = stone ~ lithography
λόγος *logos* [lŏgŏs] = word ~ logo, geology
λύρα *lyra* [loorä] = harp ~ lyre, lyrical

MY μῦ
MU M μ

The lower case *mu* can be found in the eyebrow and the nose of the gentleman with the monocle. *Monos* [mŏnŏs], meaning "single" or "only," is used as a prefix in many other words, with roots also coming from Ancient Greek: monotony (a single sound), monologue (a speech performed by one actor), monogram (initial letters of a name), and monotheism (belief in one God), etc.

The slang word megabucks borrows from the Greek word *megas* [megäs], which means "large." A small sound can be made large with a megaphone. Megalomania is a mental disorder marked by delusions of grandeur. A megaton refers to the explosive force of a million metric tons of dynamite.

Metron [metrŏn] shows up in many words for measurements: meter, millimeter, centimeter, speedometer, metric, and metronome.

The word for "mother" in Greek is *mētēr* [mātār] We find it in the English words: matriarch, maternal, and matron.

Microwave, microchip, and microscope come from the word μικρός *mikros* [meekrŏs] which means "small." We use a microscope to see small things like microbes, or germs. The human being can be described as a microcosm, a little world, in comparison to the macrocosm, the universe, formed from the Greek μακρός *makros* [mäkrŏs] for "long, lofty."

μέγας *megas* [megäs] = large ~ megaphone
μέτρον *metron* [metrŏn] = measure ~ meter
μήτηρ *mētēr* [mātār] = mother ~ maternal
μνήμη *mnēmē* [mnāmā] = memory ~ mnemonic, amnesia
μόνος *monos* [mŏnŏs] = single, only ~ monocle, monogram
μύσταξ *mystax* [moostäks] = upper lip ~ moustache

NY νῦ
NU Ν ν

The lower case *nu* is hidden in the ship five times. Three are quite obvious. The Greek word for ship is *naus* [nows]. Derivatives of it are seen in words like nautical and even navy. In the Greek myth involving Jason and the Golden Fleece, the sailors on his ship, the Ἀργώ *Argō*, were called Argonauts. With that in mind, what would "star sailors" be called? (Remember, the Russian cosmonauts were first.)

In 1898 two British chemists discovered a new gas. Later it was electrified in a glass tube, and a bright light was the result. Since the 1920s it has been used in signage advertising businesses. That may seem old, but back then, it was new, so it was given the name neon, which comes from *neos* [neŏs], the Greek word for "new."

Often "neo-" is used as a prefix denoting something new, as in the Neolithic Age, the New Stone Age. A neophyte is a person who is a beginner in some endeavor. The neonatal wing in the hospital is for the newborn babies.

The Ancient Greek word *nyx*, for "night," is descended from the same Indo-European root word as *nox* in Latin, *Nacht* in German, *noche* in Spanish and "night" in English.

ναῦς *naus* [nows] = ship ~ nautical, navy, astronaut
νέος *neos* [neŏs] = new ~ neon, neophyte
νεῦρον *neuron* [nĕūrŏn] = sinew ~ nerve, neuralgia
νίκη *nikē* [neekā] = victory ~ Nike shoes, *Nike of Samothrace*, an Ancient Greek marble sculpture now in the Louvre in Paris
νύξ *nyx* [nooks] = night

ΞΙ ξῖ
XI Ξ ξ

Xylon [ksoolŏn] is the Ancient Greek word for "wood." Our musical instrument, the xylophone, consists of a series of wooden tone bars. Xylem is the woody tissue that supports a plant stem and conducts water. (Phloem, from another Greek word φλοιός *phloios* [floyŏs] for "bark," conducts the nourishment.)

In English, the letter *x* has two pronunciations: At the beginning of a word it is usually pronounced [zee] as is the first *x* in "Xerox," and [ks] as is the last *x*. But in Greek, the letter *xi* is always pronounced [ks].

The Ancient Greek word for "strange" is *xenos* [ksenŏs]. People who fear strangers are described as being xenophobic (φόβος *phobos* [fŏbŏs] is the Greek word for "fear").

A derivative of *xenos* is another Greek word for "hospitality" or "guest friendship": ξενία *xenia* [ksenĭä]. In English, xenia is a botanical term for the positive effect on a hybrid plant brought about through receiving "foreign" pollen. Zeus is sometimes referred to as *Zeus Xenios*, meaning he was a god of, among other things, travelers.

The word for "dry" in Greek is *xeros* [ksārŏs], from which we have the word xerography, meaning dry printing, that is, without wet ink. The Xerox Corporation borrowed the Greek word in naming its dry copying process, and we have come to use the word also as a verb to mean making copies on such a machine.

ξένος *xenos* [ksenŏs] = stranger ~ xenophobia, xenon, xenia
ξηρός *xēros* [ksārŏs] = dry ~ xerography, xerox
ξύλον *xylon* [ksoolŏn] = wood ~ xylophone, xylem

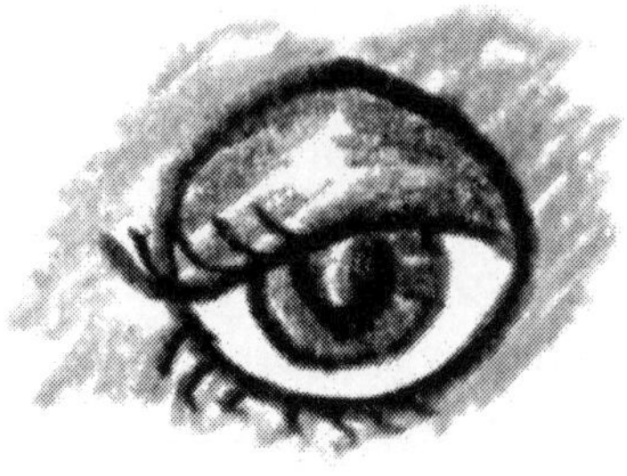

OMIKPON ὄμικρον
OMICRON Ο ο

When doctors specialize in studying the eye, they are called ophthalmologists, from the Ancient Greek word for eye, *ophthalmos* [ŏfthälmŏs]. This word is one of the few in English that has four consonants in a row. When pronouncing ophthalmology, don't forget the "ph" before the "th."

The word for "road" in Ancient Greek is *hodos* [hŏdŏs]. The device used in a car to measure the distance we travel along a road or highway is thus called an odometer. This word also shows up as a suffix, -ode, from the Greek for "way" or "path," as in electrode, a pathway for electric current.

Orthos [ŏrthŏs] is the Ancient Greek word for "straight." To align one's teeth correctly we go to an orthodontist. The word "orthodox" is also related. Orthodox thinking is generally thought to be correct thinking, or conforming to the official accepted or standard opinion.

Osteon [ŏsteŏn] is the word in Greek for "bone." A doctor who specializes in working with bones is called an osteopath. Osteoporosis is an affliction, often in old age, due to a loss of bone mass.

ὁδός *hodos* [hŏdŏs] = road ~ odometer, ode, rhapsody
ὅλος *holos* [hŏlŏs] = whole, all ~ holistic
ὀρθός *orthos* [ŏrthŏs] = straight, correct ~ orthodox, orthodontics
ὀστέον *osteon* [ŏsteŏn] = bone ~ osteopath, osteoporosis
ὀφθαλμός *ophthalmos* [ŏfthälmŏs] = eye ~ ophthalmologist

ΠΙ πι̂
PI Π π

The lower case letter *pi is* outlined in the tunic being worn by the running child in the picture. One form of the word for "child" in Ancient Greek is παιδός *paidos* [pīdŏs]. We find its distant cousin in the name for a doctor for children, a pediatrician. Pedagogue is another related word. In Ancient Greece a person assigned to be a teacher would go from house to house, leading children to a place where they would be taught.

Patēr [pätār] is the Ancient Greek word for "father." From it we get the word paternal. This can be used to indicate your grandparents on your father's side of the family. Your maternal grandparents would be from your mother's side.

In the Bible the elder ruling fathers, Abraham, Isaac, and Jacob were known as the Patriarchs of the Old Testament. Today the oldest man in a family or group can be referred to as a patriarch.

The name for "city" or "city-state" used by the Ancient Greeks was πόλις *polis* [pŏlis]. The word is evident in a number of our words: metropolis, Minneapolis and Annapolis, even police, and politics.

The word for "fire" in Ancient Greek is *pyr* [poor]. It appears in the word pyre, which is a fire for burning a body in a funeral rite. A person who has a compulsion to set fires is called a pyromaniac. Pyrex is a brand name for heat-resistant glass. And many of us enjoy a pyrotechnic display on the Fourth of July!

πᾶν *pan* [pän] = all ~ panorama, pandemonium, panacea
πατήρ *patēr* [pätār] = father ~ paternal, patriarch
πῦρ *pyr* [poor] = fire ~ pyre, pyromaniac, Pyrex, pyrotechnics

ΡΩ ῥῶ
RHO Ρ ρ

Rhinos [hrĭnŏs] is the Ancient Greek word for "of the nose." The capital letter looks like our capital *P*. The lower case looks like a cursive *p*. Look for it in the nostril and lower part of the nose in the cartoon drawing. Some people with a nose that size opt for plastic surgery. The technical term for that is rhinoplasty, otherwise known as a "nose job."

The rhinoceros got its name from the large horn on its nose. *Keras* κέρας is the word for "horn," so a rhinoceros is literally a "nose-horn." Often the animal's name is abbreviated rhino.

You may wonder about the *h* in *rho*, in "rhinoceros," and in "rhinoplasty." The rough breathing symbol is always present when the *rho* is at the beginning of a word. In pronouncing *rhinos*, make an *h* sound along with the *r* sound: [hr].

Rhythmos [hroothmŏs], meaning "measured repetition," has this similar characteristic. Related words include rhythm, arithmetic, and eurythmy.

ῥήτωρ *rhētōr* [hrātōr] = speaker ~ rhetoric
ῥίς *rhis* [hrĭs] = nose
ῥίνος *rhinos* [hrĭnŏs] = of the nose ~ rhinoceros
ῥυθμός *rhythmos* [hroothmŏs] = measured repetition ~ rhythm, arithmetic, eurythmy

ΣΙΓΜΑ σῖγμα SIGMA Σ σ ς

This letter has the unique feature of having two different lower case forms. When *sigma* appears at the end of a word, the form used is ς, similar to our letter *s*. The main difference is that the top curve of the form is larger than the lower. When *sigma* appears elsewhere in a word, the Greek letter is σ, which form can be seen in the pictograph of the crying baby's mouth.

The word for "mouth" in Greek is *stoma* [stŏmä]. An obviously related word is <u>stoma</u>ch, which is a rather large mouth. However, <u>stoma</u> is a word in itself in English. On the backside of leaves are microscopic oval structures that open and close, breathing in carbon dioxide and breathing out oxygen. These tiny pores or "mouths" are called <u>stomas</u>.

The tent-like building used as a backdrop in Ancient Greek drama was called a *skēnē* [skānā]. From it the word <u>scene</u> was formed.

We know "Sophia" as a female name; it means "wisdom" in Ancient Greek. We find it in our word philo<u>sophy</u>. The first part of this word comes from one of the words in Greek for "love": φιλία *philia* [fileeä]. Thus <u>philosophy</u> is the "love of wisdom." Closely related is the Greek word *sophos*, which means "skilled" or "clever." We see this in <u>sophis</u>ticated, meaning "having acquired worldly knowledge or refinement." It also appears in the word <u>sopho</u>more. The last part of the word comes from μωρόν *mōron*, meaning "foolish." So a sophomore, a second-year high school or college student who might think he or she knows everything, is actually a "wise or clever fool."

σκηνή *skēnē* [skānā] = tent ~ scene
σοφία *sophia* [sŏfeeä] = wisdom ~ philosophy, sophomore
σοφός *sophos* [sŏfŏs] = skilled ~ sophisticated
στόμα *stoma* [stŏmä] = mouth ~ stomach

TAY ταῦ
TAU Τ τ

The letter *tau* is pictured in the drawing of a rock hammer, a technical tool used by geologists for chipping rocks for analysis. It takes some skill or craft to do this well, which leads us to the word technique. This word's ancestor is *technē* [tekhnā], meaning "craft" or "art." As the hammer is a tool, it also suggests other related words: technology, technical, technician and even the slang word "techie."

"Bull" in Ancient Greek is *tauros* [towrŏs]. The starry constellation Taurus derives its name from this word. It also is part of the word minotaur, the half-bull monster of King Minos' labyrinth in Greek mythology.

Topos [tŏpŏs], the Greek word for "place," is an ancient cousin of our word topography, which can refer to the surface of the place around us. A topographical map is one that shows the lay of the land, often including its elevation. If a medicine is to be used topically, it is not to be taken internally, but used only on the surface of the skin. A topic or theme is the subject of a speech, essay or conversation, a common place to start.

ταῦρος *tauros* [towrŏs] = bull ~ Taurus, minotaur
τάξις *taxis* [taksis] = order, arrangement ~ taxonomy, taxidermy
τέχνη *technē* [tekhnā] = craft, art ~ technique, technical
τόπος *topos* [tŏpŏs] = place ~ topic, topography

ΥΨΙΛΟΝ ὑψιλόν
UPSILON Υ υ

The word for "water" in Ancient Greek is *hydor* [hoodōr]. From it we get the word hydrant. The little drop of water coming from the hydrant is in the shape of the lower case *upsilon*. To hydrate oneself is to drink a sufficient amount of water. One of the major contents of water is hydrogen. Hydroelectric power is energy generated by running water.

If a person is described as "hyper," short for hyperactive, it means that person is overactive. The Greek word for "over" or "above" is *hyper* [hooper]. A hyperbole [hīperbōlee] is a figure of speech in which exaggeration is used to make a point. I've told you a thousand times what a hyperbole is.

The opposite of *hyper* is *hypo* [hoopŏ], meaning "below" or "under." To be hypoactive is to be sluggish. The Greek for "skin" is δέρμα *derma* [dermä], so we call a needle that is used to inject substances into the body under the skin a hypodermic. Someone whose blood sugar is too low is hypoglycemic.

ὑγίεια *hygieia* [hoogiää] = health ~ hygiene
ὕδωρ *hydor* [hoodōr] = water ~ hydrant, hydrogen
ὑπέρ *hyper* [hooper] = over, above ~ hyperbole, hyperactive
ὑπό *hypo* [hoopŏ] = under ~ hypodermic, hypoglycemia

ΦΙ φῖ
PHI Φ φ

Put a hand on your throat where your larynx or "voice box" is and say something; *phi* will do. Feel the vibration? The larynx consists of a pair of vocal cords through which air passes, creating sound. With a little imagination, look at the illustration: picture the two vocal cords on either side of the vertical line, which represents the air passing between them.

The word for "speech" or "voice" in Ancient Greek is *phōnē* [fōnā]. Besides telephone, phonetics, and phonograph, other related words include symphony (sounding together) and euphony (pleasing, good sound), and cacophony (unpleasant or too much sound).

Philia [fileeä], one of the Greek words for "love," was mentioned earlier in connection with philosophy. When combined with the Greek word for "brother," ἀδελφός *adelphos* [ädelfŏs], it reveals the name and the motto for the large Pennsylvania metropolis, Philadelphia, "The City of Brotherly Love."

"To carry" or "to bear" in Greek is *pherō* [ferō]. The legend of St. Christopher describes a ferryman bearing the Christ child across a river on his shoulders (as pictured on the St. Christopher medal). The *ph* is often transliterated as *f*, as in conifer, a cone-bearing tree.

The word for "nature" in Greek is *physis* [foosis]. From it we get the word physics, the science of matter and energy (natural laws). It is also the source for our words physical, physician, and physique, the natural proportions of one's features.

φέρω *phero* [ferō] = to carry, bear ~ Christopher, conifer
φιλία *philia* [fileeä] = love ~ philosophy
φύσις *physis* [foosis] = nature ~ physics, physical
φωνή *phōnē* [fōnā] = speech, voice ~ telephone, phonetics

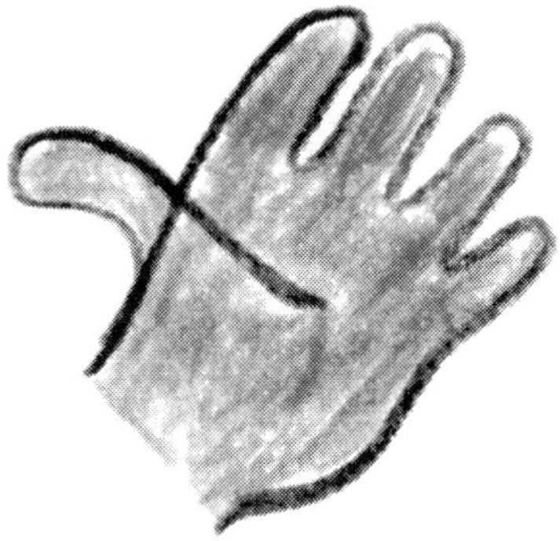

XI χῖ
CHI Χ χ

A <u>chiro</u>practor does not use drugs in working with a patient, only the hands. For this reason I chose to use the image of a hand to introduce the letter that is the initial letter of the word "hand" in Ancient Greek: *cheir* [khār]. The letter *chi* is sounded [kh] as in the Scottish word for "lake": *loch.*

The number 1000 in Greek is *chilioi* [khileeoy]. English relatives include <u>kilo</u>meter (a thousand meters, or about three-fifths of a mile), <u>kilo</u>gram (a thousand grams, or about 2.25 pounds), and <u>kilo</u>watt, a thousand watts, the unit of measure that power companies use to dispense and charge for electricity.

One word for "time" in Ancient Greek is *chronos* [khrŏnŏs]. From that association we get a number of time-related words: <u>chrono</u>logy, <u>chrono</u>logical, and <u>chrono</u>meter, an extremely precise timepiece. When one has had a continuing medical problem, it is called a <u>chronic</u> ailment or condition.

A very closely related Greek word, χρονικά [khrŏnikä] *chronika,* means "an account of historical events in order," and we see it in the titles for the well-known literary tales, *The Chronicles of Narnia* of C.S. Lewis and *The Martian Chronicles* by Ray Bradbury, as well as the Old Testament history books, the First and Second Chronicles.

The words <u>chrome</u>, <u>chrom</u>atic and <u>chromo</u>some all derive from the Greek word for "color": *chrōma* [khrōmä].

χείρ *cheir* [khār] = hand ~ chiropractor
χίλιοι *chilioi* [khileeoy] = thousand ~ kilometer, kilogram
χρόνος *chronos* [khrŏnŏs] = time ~ chronology, chronic
χρῶμα *chrōma* [khrōmä] = color ~ chromatic

ΨΙ ψι̂
PSI Ψ ψ

In English words beginning with *ps*, the *p* is silent, as in psychology and the Old Testament book of Psalms. But pronunciations of the Greek all begin with *ps*. (The Greeks can still pronounce it, even if we can't!) We have an echo of it when we want to get someone's attention quietly: "Psst."

We know the poems in the Psalms were meant to be sung because the Greek word *psalmos* [psälmŏs] means "song."

A psaltery is not a well-known musical instrument, but it serves well to illustrate the Greek letter. It was an ancient stringed instrument that was played to accompany the reading or singing of the Psalms, and a psalter is a collection of Psalms.

Pseudēs [psĕūdās] is the Greek word for "false." An author who wants to remain anonymous can use a false name called a pseudonym. A pseudo-intellectual is someone pretending to be smarter than he or she really is. Biologists speak of amoebas having pseudopodia, little false feet, with which they move about.

Our word psychology comes from the Greek word for "soul" or "spirit": *psychē* [psookhā]. Thus a psychologist, who deals with mental and emotional processes, can be thought of as a sort of doctor for the soul. We call someone with special mental powers such as ESP a psychic. And the slang expression to psych someone out means to "mess with their mind."

ψαλμός *psalmos* [psälmŏs] = song ~ Psalms, psalter
ψευδής *pseudēs* [psĕūdās] = false ~ pseudonym, pseudopod
ψυχή *psychē* [psookhā] = spirit, soul ~ psychic, psychology

ΩΜΕΓΑ ὠμέγα
OMEGA Ω ω

The *omega* is the letter used to express a long *o* sound. The lower case Greek letter resembles the English lower case *w*. The capital *omega* can be seen in the pictograph surrounding the old-fashioned mantle clock, chosen because one word that begins with *omega* is *hōra* [hōrä], which means "time" or "season," and from which we get the word hour. Horology is the science of measuring time or the art of making timepieces.

It is curious that these Greek words have rough breathing symbols on the *omegas* and so the *h* is sounded. Yet when we use their English derivatives, the *h* is silent.

A little-known word, horary, is also related. It means "hourly." When we say "horary" we sound the *h*. The *h* is also sounded in horoscope, meaning literally "looking at the hour," or as we use it today, a diagram of the position of the planets and stars at a given point in time, usually one's birth.

Because *omega* is the last letter in the Greek alphabet, it is sometimes used to mean just that: the end. Often it is paired with the *alpha*, for the beginning. As such, they express the "beginning and ending" of something. In the New Testament *the Alpha and the Omega* refers to the Christ, or God's Love as the beginning and end of all things.

ὥρα *hōra* [hōrä] = time, season ~ hour, horoscope, horary
ὠμέγα *ōmega* [ōmĕgä] = the last, the end ~ Omega watches, the "last word" in timekeeping

And now we have come to the end of this chapter.

4. GREEK NUMBERS FROM 1–20

Arithmoi - 'Αριθμοί

	Greek	Transliteration [Pronunciation]	Derivatives
0	μηδέν	*mēden* [māden]	
1	εἷς, ἕν	*heis* [hās], *hen* [hen]	ace
2	δύο	*duo* [dooō]	duet, dual
3	τρεῖς	*treis* [trās]	tricycle, triple
4	τέτταρες	*tettares* [tetäres]	tetrahedron
5	πέντε	*pente* [pentĕ]	pentathlon
6	ἕξ	*heks* [hex]	hexagon
7	ἑπτά	*hepta* [heptä]	heptagon
8	ὀκτώ	*oktō* [ŏktō]	octopus
9	ἐννέα	*ennea* [ĕnnĕä]	ennead
10	δέκα	*deka* [dekä]	decade
11	ἕνδεκα	*hendeka* [hendekä]	hendecagon
12	δώδεκα	*dōdeka* [dōdekä]	dodecahedron
13	τρεῖς καὶ δέκα*	*treis kai deka* [trās kī dekä]	
14	τέτταρες καὶ δέκα	*tettareskaideka* [tetäres kī dekä]	
15	πεντεκαίδεκα	*pentekaideka* [pentĕkīdekä]	
16	ἑκκαίδεκα	*hekkaideka* [hekīdekä]	
17	ἑπτακαίδεκα	*heptkaideka* [heptäkīdekä]	
18	ὀκτωκαίδεκα	*oktōkaideka* [ŏktōkīdekä]	
19	ἐννεακαίδεκα	*enneakaideka* [ennĕäkīdekä]	
20	εἴκοσι	*eikose* [ākŏsee]	icosahedron

*Καί is Greek for "and." Thus "thirteen" is written τρεῖς καὶ δέκα: "three and ten." Fourteen is: τέτταρες καὶ δέκα: "four and ten," and so forth, up to nineteen. From fifteen on, the three separate words are written as one.

5.
Reading Ancient Greek

Now that we are more familiar with the Greek alphabet and some words in Greek and their English derivatives, you may ask if it is possible to read this marvelous language. Let's give it a try. Below are some excerpts from philosophy and literature, presented first in Ancient Greek, then transliterated into English with a pronunciation guide, followed by translation into English.

Philosophical Sayings

From a civilization famed for its influence on Western philosophy, it is appropriate to list a few wise sayings from this rich tradition.

Γνῶθι Σαυτόν. *Gnōthi Sauton* [Gnōthee Sowtŏn]
Know Thyself.

Μηδὲν Ἄγαν. *Mēden Agan* [Māden Agän]
Nothing in Excess. (Literally: Nothing too much.)

Μέτρον ἄριστον. *Metron ariston* [Metrŏn aristŏn]
Moderation in all things. (Literally: The middle is best.)

Μελέτη τὸ πᾶν. *Meletē to pan.* [Meletā tŏ pän]
Practice makes perfect. (Literally: Practice is everything.)

Πάντων Χρημάτων Μέτρον Ἄνθρωπος.
Pantōn Chrēmatōn Metron Anthrōpos.
[Păntōn Khrāmätōn Metrŏn Anthrōpŏs]
The human being is the measure of all things.

Εὕρηκα! *Heurēka!* [Hĕūrākä]: I found it! or, I have it!

Πάντα Ῥεῖ. *Panta Rhei* [Päntä Hrā]: All is flowing.

The First Lines of "The Odyssey"

by the poet Homer, ca. 700 BC

Homer, the great poet who wrote *The Iliad* and *The Odyssey*, composed these two masterpieces in hexameter. As one recites the lines in Greek, it is possible to step that rhythm for each line.

ΟΔΨΣΣΕΙΑ

Ἄνδρα μοι ἔννεπε, Μοῦσα, πολύτροπον, ὃς μάλα πολλὰ
πλάγχθη, ἐπεὶ Τροίης ἱερὸν πτολίεθρον ἔπερσεν,
πολλῶν δ' ἀνθρώπων ἴδεν ἄστεα καὶ νόον ἔγνω,
πολλὰ δ' ὅ γ' ἐν πόντῳ πάθεν ἄλγεα ὃν κατὰ θυμόν,
ἀρνύμενος ἥν τε ψυχὴν καὶ νόστον ἑταίρων.

Andra moi ennepe, Mousa, polytropon, hos mala polla
plangthē, epei Troiēs hieron ptoliethron epersen,
pollōn d'anthrōpōn iden astea kai noon egnō,
polla d'ho g'en pontō pathen, algea hon kata thumon,
arnumenos hēn te psychēn kai noston hetairōn.

[Andrä moi enepe, Moosä, pŏlootrŏpŏn, hŏs mälä pŏlä
plängthā, epā Troyās hīerŏn ptoliĕthrŏn epersen,
pŏllōn d' änthrōpōn eeden ästĕä kī nŏŏn egnō,
pŏllä d'hŏ g'en pŏntō päthen älgĕä hŏn kätä thoomŏn,
arnoomenŏs hān te psookhān kī nŏstŏn hetīrōn.]

Tell me, O Muse, of the man of many devices, who wandered full many ways after he had sacked the sacred citadel of Troy. Many were the men whose cities he saw and whose mind he learned, aye, and many the woes he suffered in his heart, upon the sea, seeking to win his own life and the return of his comrades.

The Prayer to Zeus

Ο Ζεὺς, πρὸς γὰρ θεοῦ
εἴμεν ξεῖνοι τε πτωχοί τε,
ἀλλὰ Ζεὺς πάντων
ὁράει τέλος.

O Zeus, pros gar theou
eimen xeinoi te ptōxoi te,
alla Zeus pantōn
horaei telos.

[O Dzĕūs, prŏs gar thĕoo
āmen ksānoy te ptōkhoy te,
älä Dzĕūs päntōn
horäā telŏs.]

O Zeus, facing towards god
we are both strangers and beggars,
for Zeus alone of all the gods
sees our final destination.

This prayer is often attributed to Solon Σόλων [Sŏlōn] (ca. 640–558 BC), an Athenian statesman and lawgiver, considered one of the Seven Sages of Greece. His writings on government strongly influenced James Madison in shaping the U.S. Constitution.

In Waldorf schools this invocation is often spoken by the students to open the fifth grade pentathlon event.

NEW TESTAMENT GREEK AND THE FIRST LINES OF THE GOSPEL OF JOHN

Attic Greek was spoken in the region of Attica, of which Athens was the premier city. It was the tongue of Plato, Aristotle, the dramatists whose works have survived, and many historians, including Xenophon and Thucydides. As with all languages, Attic Greek changed over time. Hundreds of years later, when the New Testament was written in Greek, the language had indeed changed—to the degree that it was given a new name. New Testament Greek is known as Koine [koynā] Greek. It differs from classical Attic Greek in some ways, much like the way that American English and even modern British English vary from the Elizabethan English of Shakespeare and of the King James Version of the Bible in the 1600s. John's Gospel, Chapter I, verses 1–5 appears in Koine Greek as follows:

'Εν ἀρχῇ ἦν ὁ Λόγος, καὶ ὁ Λόγος ἦν
πρὸς τὸν Θεόν, καὶ Θεὸς ἦν ὁ Λόγος.
οὗτος ἦν ἐν ἀρχῇ πρὸς τὸν Θεόν.
Πάντα δι' αὐτοῦ ἐγένετο·
καὶ χωρὶς αὐτοῦ ἐγένετο οὐδὲ ἕν ὅ γέγονεν.
'Εν αὐτῷ ζωὴ ἦν,
καὶ ἡ ζωὴ ἦν τὸ φῶς τῶν ἀνθρώπων.
Καὶ τὸ φῶς ἐν τῇ σκοτὶα φαίνει,
καὶ ἡ σκοτία αυτὸ οὐ κατέλαβεν.

En archē ēn ho Logos, kai ho Logos ēn
pros ton Theon, kai Theos ēn ho Logos.
Houtos ēn en archē pros ton Theon.
Panta di' autou egeneto;
kai chōris autou egeneto oude hen ho gegonen.
En autō zōē ēn,
kai hē zōē ēn to phōs tōn anthrōpōn.
Kai to phōs en tē skotia phainei,
kai hē skotia auto ou katelaben.

[En ärchā ān hŏ Lŏgŏs, kī hŏ Lŏgŏs ān
prŏs tŏn Thĕŏn, kī Thĕos ān hŏ Lŏgŏs.
Hootŏs ān en ärkhā prŏs tŏn Thĕŏn.
Päntä di' owtoo egenetŏ;
kī khōris owtoo egenetŏ oode hen hŏ gegŏnen.
En owtō zōā ān,
kī hä zōā ān tŏ phōs tōn änthrōpōn.
Kī tŏ phōs en tā skŏtiä finā,
kī hā skŏtiä owtŏ oo käteläben.]

In the beginning was the Word, and
the Word was with God, and the Word was God.
He was in the beginning with God.
All things were made through Him;
and without Him was not anything made that was made.
In Him was life,
and the life was the light of men.
The light shines in darkness,
and the darkness has not overcome it.
(Revised Standard Version)

The Acropolis Today

6.
More English Words with Ancient Greek Origins

Greek word	Transliterated	English meaning	Related words
ἀγορά	*agora*	marketplace	agoraphobia
αἰών	*aiōn*	age, time	aeon, eon
ἄλγος	*algos*	pain	neuralgia, analgesic
ἀμφί	*amphi*	on both sides of	amphibian
ἄνθρωπος	*anthrōpos*	human being	anthropology
ἀργύριον	*argurion*	silver	Argentina
ἀριθμός	*arithmos*	number	arithmetic
ἄριστος	*aristos*	best	aristocratic
ἀρχή	*archē*	beginning	archaic
ἄρχων	*archōn*	leader	patriarch
βάθος	*bathos*	depth	bathysphere
βασιλικός	*basilikos*	royal, kingly	basilica
βουκόλος	*boukolos*	cowherd	bucolic
γάμος	*gamos*	marriage	polygamy
γυνή	*gunē*	woman	gynecology
δαίμων	*daimōn*	deity	demon, daimon
δένδρον	*dendron*	tree, shrub	rhododendron
δεύτερος	*deuteros*	second	Deuteronomy
διά	*dia*	through	diameter
διδακτός	*didaktos*	teachable	didactic
δόξα	*doxa*	opinion	dogma, doxology
δρόμος	*dromos*	chariot race course	syndrome, hippodrome
δῶρον	*dōron*	gift	Dorothy, Theodore

ἔθνος	*ethnos*	nation, tribe	ethnic
ἐκ	*ek*	out of, from	ecstasy, exit
ἕλιξ	*helix*	spiral shape	helix
ἐπίγραμμα	*epigramma*	inscription	epigram
ἐπιφάνεια	*epiphaneia*	manifestation	epiphany
ἔργον	*ergon*	work	erg, urge
ἡγεμών	*hēgemōn*	leader, guide	hegemony
ἠχέω	*ēcheō*	resound	echo
θάνατος	*thanatos*	death	"Thanatopsis"
θέμα	*thema*	composition	theme
ἴσος	*isos*	equally	isometrics
κακός	*kakos*	badly, ill	cacophony
κινέω	*kineō*	to move	kinetic, kinesthetic
κλίνω	*klinō*	to slope	incline, decline
κρανίον	*kranion*	skull	cranium
κριτής	*kritēs*	judge	critic
κύκλος	*kuklos*	circle	cycle, Cyclops
λαβύρινθος	*labyrinthos*	winding maze	labyrinth
λευκός	*leukos*	white	leukemia, leucocyte
μανία	*mania*	madness, frenzy	maniac, manic
μάντις	*mantis*	seer	mantis, praying mantis
μέγιστος	*megistos*	greatest	majestic, majesty
μέλας	*melas*	black, dark	melancholic
μετά	*meta*	beyond	metaphysics
μυρίος	*myrios*	countless	myriad
νεκρός	*nekros*	corpse	necromancy, necrology
οἶκος	*oikos*	house	ecology, economy
ὀλίγος	*oligos*	few	oligarchy
ὁμός	*homos*	one and the same	homogeneous

ὄνομα	*onoma*	name	nominate
ὄρνις	*ornis*	bird	ornithology
ὀρχήστρα	*orchēstra*	space for dancing	orchestra
οὐρανός	*ouranos*	sky, heaven	Uranus
πάλαι	*palai*	long ago	Paleolithic
παρά	*para*	beside	parallel, parable
περί	*peri*	around	perimeter
πέτρα	*petra*	rock	petrified, petroleum
πλευρά	*pleura*	rib, side	pleurisy
πλῆθος	*plēthos*	a great number	plethora
πλουτέω	*pluteō*	to be wealthy	plutocrat
ποίημα	*poiēma*	anything made	poem
πόλεμος	*polemos*	war	polemic
πολύς	*polys*	many	polygon, polyglot
πομπή	*pompē*	procession	pomp, pompous
πόρος	*poros*	means of passing	pores, porous
πρᾶγμα	*pragma*	business-like	pragmatic
πρεσβύτερος	*presbyteros*	elder	Presbyterian
πρό	*pro*	before	provide
πτέρυξ	*pteryx*	wing	pterodactyl
ῥόδον	*rhodon*	rose	rose, rhododendron
σάρξ	*sarx*	flesh	sarcasm, sarcophagus
σατράπης	*satrapēs*	governor	satrap
σεισμός	*seismos*	earthquake	seismograph
σημαίνω	*sēmainō*	to give a signal	semaphore
σκέπτομαι	*skeptomai*	to inquire	skeptic
σκόπος	*skopos*	look to see	scope
στάδιον	*stadion*	600 Greek feet	stadium
στενός	*stenos*	narrow	stent, stenographer
στρατηγός	*stratēgos*	commander	strategy
σύμβολον	*symbolon*	sign, watchword	symbol
σχίζω	*schizo*	to split	schizoid, schism
σῶμα	*sōma*	body, person	psychosomatic
σωτηρία	*sōtēria*	salvation	soteriology

τάλαντον	*talanton*	balance weight, sum	talent
τείνω	*teinō*	to stretch	tense, tension
τῆλε	*tēle*	faraway	telephone, telegraph
τέλος	*telos*	goal, destination	teleology
τρόπος	*tropos*	turn, direction	troposphere
τύραννος	*tyrannos*	absolute sovereign	tyrant
φαίνω	*phainō*	to appear	epiphany
φάλαγξ	*phalanx*	line of battle	phalanx
φάρμακον	*pharmakon*	drug, poison	pharmacy
φεύγω	*pheugō*	to flee	fugitive
φόβος	*phobos*	fear	phobia
φῶς	*phōs*	light	phosphorus, photograph
χάος	*chaos*	chaos	chaos, chaotic
χάρις	*charis*	grace	charisma, Eucharist
χάσμα	*chasma*	deep, division	chasm
χορδή	*chordē*	gut-string	cord
ὦσμος	*ōsmos*	a pushing	osmosis

7.
The Mysteries and Curiosities of the Alphabet

The alphabet as we know it in Western civilization has a long, evolved history. General opinion holds that it came out of ancient Phoenicia where a standardized phonetic system of letters was developed. The Greeks, who traded with this sea-going society in the region that is now Lebanon, adopted much of what was written and adapted it for their own use by about 775 BC. The fact that an alphabet has lasted for over 2700 years is no small feat!

The original meanings of the letter names were lost when the alphabet was adapted for Greek. For example, *alpha* comes from the Phoenician *aleph* (ox) and *beta* from *beth* (house). At first there were a number of different versions used in the various Greek city-states. But by early the 4th century BC they were all using the same. The lower case letters came into use around 800 AD, having been developed from Byzantine cursive writing.

Interestingly, the original direction of writing was from right to left, imitating the Phoenician practice. By the 5th century BC the direction was changed to from left to right.

The Miracle of Written Sounds

Greek or otherwise, the alphabet is a marvelous phenomenon. To take the sounds of a spoken language and represent them with visual symbols that can be read aloud or silently and produce meaning—that is amazing if not miraculous.

The ability to record and preserve stories and information has proved invaluable. Nonetheless, there are drawbacks to such a practice. When everything could be written down, a person no longer needed to memorize anything important. Thus the skill of memorizing, that had long been cultivated, weakened and sometimes was even lost. The upside, on the other hand—most would agree—has long outweighed the importance of memorization. With the alphabet and the words it can produce, a person can study a text, a passage, a lineage and memorize it at one's leisure—instead of through the painstaking rigor of listening to a bard or record keeper.

Yet there is still a place for learning "by heart." What might begin as something merely memorized by rote can grow over time and unfold its deeper, heartfelt meaning.

Learning passages of Attic or Koine Greek spoken and written hundreds and hundreds of years ago is also a way we can reach across the ages and connect with ancient lore and wisdom, taking into ourselves a common memory of Western culture. Written and memorized passages from ancient, or even modern times, can also serve as centering mantras. Wise seers have long seen the value of using a mantra for personal spiritual development.

The Curious Arrangement of Letters in the Greek and English Alphabets

The vowels and consonants that make up Greek and English have an interesting sequence in their respective alphabets. In music one speaks of "intervals" as the arrangement of various notes on a major musical scale. To speak of the interval of a "third" is to refer to a note that follows on the third note above (or below) a previous note. Thus an interval of a third from middle C would be E (CdE). A third above E is G. Likewise, a fifth from the note A is E (AbcdE). If you prefer the "do re mi" references, a third from "do" would be "mi," a fifth would be "sol," and a seventh would be "ti."

Utilizing this terminology, let us look at the Greek and English alphabets and capitalize the vowels to point out their intervals.

Α β γ δ **Ε** ζ **Η** θ **Ι** κ λ μ ν ξ **Ο** π ρ σ τ **U** φ χ ψ **Ω**

The vowels are in the following sequence: Alpha to Epsilon is a fifth (interval), Epsilon to Eta is a third, Eta to Iota is also a third. Iota to Omicron is a seventh, Omicron to Upsilon is a sixth, and Upsilon to Omega is a fifth.

In the English alphabet the vowel sequence is as follows:

A b c d **E** f g h **I** j k l m n **O** p q r s t **U** v w x y z

A to E is a fifth, and E to I is also a fifth. However, between I and O is a seventh, and from O to U is a seventh. Unlike the Greek alphabet, the English alphabet does not have a vowel for the ending letter. Nonetheless, if the curious person were to count out the interval between the U back to the A at beginning of the alphabet, that interval is a seventh.

Why is this information given? What's the point? First, it could be of interest to a musician. It implies a certain musical/rhythmical quality to the alphabet. I leave it here as a curiosity, for your contemplation.

Much more could be said about other interesting aspects of both alphabets, but this book is just an introduction. If one wants to learn more fascinating thoughts about the subject, I recommend a small booklet of a lecture by Rudolf Steiner entitled "The Alphabet, An Expression of the Mystery of Man," given in Dornach, Switzerland, on December 18, 1921, translated by V.E. Watkin, and available from Mercury Press. Rudolf Steiner was a scientist and philosopher in the early 1900s in Germany, and the founder of Waldorf education, biodynamic agriculture, and a number of other practical applications of his philosophy.

The Parthenon Today

RESOURCES

Ancient Greek, Gavin Betts & Alan Henry, London: Hodder Education, 1989 and 2003.

Beginning Greek, a Functional Approach, Stephen W. Paine, New York: Oxford University Press, 1961.

The Compact Version of the Oxford English Dictionary, New York: Oxford University Press, 1971.

English Words from Latin and Greek Elements, Donald M. Ayers, Tucson, AZ: The University of Arizona Press, 1986.

Greek-English Lexicon, Henry George Liddell & Robert Scott, 7th edition, Oxford: Clarendon Press, 1889, 1975.

An Introduction to Greek, Henry Lamar Crosby & John Nevin Schaeffer, New York: Allyn and Bacon, 1928 and 1949; recently republished by Mineola, NY: Dover Publications, Inc. (This book was my original introduction to Greek when I studied Greek at the University of Texas. It has been my main resource book. I still have my original, now rather tattered, 1949 version.)

The New Lexicon Webster's Dictionary of the English Language, New York: Lexicon Publications, Inc., 1989.

The New Testament in the Original Greek, Brooke Foss Westcott, DD, & Fenton John Anthony Hort, DD, New York: The Macmillan Publishing Co., 1925.

1000 Mythological Characters, Edward S. Ellis, New York: Hinds, Noble & Eldredge, 1899.

Webster's New Collegiate Dictionary, Springfield, MA: G&C Merriam Co., Publishers, 1953.

Webster's Seventh New Collegiate Dictionary, Springfield, MA: G&C Merriam Co., Publishers, 1963.

www.s-e-t-s.org.uk, online transliteration chart.

Photo Credits

Cover: A *Reading from Homer,* Sir Lawrence Alma-Tadema. Oil on canvas, 1885, 36⅛ × 72¼ inches (91.8 × 183.5 cm), Philadelphia Museum of Art: The George W. Elkins Collection, 1924, permission courtesy of Philadephia Museum of Art.

The Acropolis p6: rendering by Leo von Klenze, 1846, Neue Pinakothek (Gallery), Munich.

The Parthenon p8 top: Centennial Park, Nashville, TN.
The Parthenon p8 bottom: rendering by Gorham P. Stevens, 1938, pantherfile.uwm.edu/prec/www/source/mythology/0500/athena.htm, copyright 2005, permission courtesy of Bruce Precourt.

The Acropolis Today p52 both views: www.Greece-Athens.com, permission courtesy of Alexandros Damigos, Marinet Ltd.

The Parthenon Today p60: Parthenon, Athens, Greece, photo taken 1978, OPartenon de Atenas.jpg, author: Steve Swayne.

The author p63 and back cover: Andre Deslauriers, info@starsandcinema.

Compact Disc Credits

Recording engineers: Scott Waters and Andre Deslauriers
Reproduction: Bill Ernst, MauiDiscs.com
Label design: Ann Erwin

ABOUT THE AUTHOR

Keith McCrary was born and reared in New Mexico. His college education at The University of Texas in Austin included the classical languages with a major in liberal arts. Keith received a Master of Divinity from Pacific School of Religion in Berkeley, CA. He was the pastor of the First United Methodist Church in San Francisco from 1966–1969, a time and place of fascinating change in world culture.

Keith has also been a freelance artist, specializing in cartoon portraits. Over the years he has drawn over 100,000 caricatures in places like Fisherman's Wharf in San Francisco, Carnaby Street in London, and at numerous conventions on the island of Maui.

His primary employment, however, has been as a Waldorf educator. In that capacity, he has been a Class Teacher grades one through eight for twenty-nine years and has introduced Ancient Greek (and Latin) to several hundred elementary, high school and adult students. He also taught history and English to high school students for four years.

Since 1991 he has resided on the island of Maui in Hawaii. There he is the director and a major teacher with Adult Waldorf Education (AWE), a part-time teacher training institute, which he helped to found in 1996.

Keith has been described as a master teacher, a wordsmith, a philologist (a lover of words), a humorist and an inveterate punster. In his "retiring" years, he has visited, taught, and mentored in schools in Mexico, Japan and the United States.

Besides teaching, writing and drawing, Keith's main artistic passion is improvisational dance. He has done some serious choreography, especially for some compositions of Igor Stravinsky.

Keith and his wife, Lynette, have one daughter, four sons and, at the time of this writing, eight grandchildren.

Dedication

To David Mitchell, long time director of AWSNA Publications, who grasped the vision of this book back in 2002 and patiently waited ten years for the manuscript. This book is dedicated in memory of a dear and good friend.

To Ann Erwin, who also waited patiently and with continued support, encouragement and enthusiasm for the project. It is largely due to her dilgence, mellow perseverance and hard work that this book is in your hands.

To the hundreds of Greek students in several Waldorf schools, who taught me much by going along for the journey.

Acknowledgements

Thanks go to Anjte M. Bojarsky for lending me a number of resource books, as did Coral Cottage.

Thanks also go to Genie Sakaguchi and Donald Samson for proofing the manuscript and making suggestions. Donald's impressive knowledge of and experience with Greek and his caring for the project have made a significant contribution to the book.

My attitude of gratitude includes my daughter, Renee Kirk, who strongly encouraged me over the years to do this project.

And finally, my appreciation extends to my wife, Lynette McCrary, for her steadfastness through it all.

67180736R00037

Made in the USA
Charleston, SC
06 February 2017